I0163397

Veil: The Little Foxes

By Justin Loretta

Veil

Veil: The Little Foxes was created from the imagination of Justin Huling. Any subject, person or scenario that replicates 'reality' or 'real life' is strictly coincidental. Copyright© 2011 by Justin Huling. All rights reserved.

Production Credit

All words and formatting were provided by Justin Huling.

Cover photo by Cason Norman.

Special thanks to John Mallozzi.

ISBN 978-1-257-77391-6

Veil

The deeper that sorrow carves into your being, the more joy you can contain.

Is not the cup that holds your wine the very cup that was burned in the potter's oven?

And is not the lute that soothes your spirit, the very wood that was hollowed with knives?

When you are joyous, look deep into your heart and you shall find it is only that which has given you sorrow that is giving you joy.

-Kahlil Gibran

Veil

For my Brothers

Veil: The Little Foxes

Veil

Lot

Night

Awash

Veil

I Halve

Bastard

Mirage

Oh, Monster

Insha'Allah

Storms

Quandary

(A)Part

They Ran

Stobbit

Twister

Negative

Boga

Grandfather

Veil

Beam

Magpie

Dreams

Relieve

Veil

Lot

The rays come dancing

And upon impact, shatter.

Wet, newborn eyes, revealing

Our mothers diamond skin.

Shimmer, that sun seer

Whispered to the wind.

In brogue long forgotten

And echoing within.

The woman, wheat

Listening discreet.

Really, just a passerby

Retreat, retreat;

Overheard, an ancient word

The archaic seal cracks.

Golden lotus, blooming still

While fierce flames attack.

Veil

Night

I am sound,

Like baby sleep

Drifting off to blackness

On magic carpet sheets.

Starless, Elysian veil, sail

Onward, somnolent sea;

Horizon-thin black line

Impale, approaching dawn.

Free to flee.

Veil

Awash

Calm and fluid

An eddy, and as temporary.

A day, a year. Sigh.

It doesn't matter here.

Everything else cannot

Restrict its inertia

And slips from caught

Through my hands,

"Like so much water."

Like so much sand.

Veil

Veil

Lost in the rush

Of post war apocalypse

Technology push.

Scattered and abandoned,

All but forgotten

Generation. Rotten

Legs to stand on,

Wandering hopeless, cynical

Following cheap, innumerable idols.

All equally worthless

And a different color.

Veil

I halve

A nap.

On my lap, the screen

An unshaded window

Light draft, cracked.

It becomes weightless

I fall away from it

And my body; sometimes

It does not want to return

To my sinews and bones

And moans when I crack

The whip over its stern

The heavy velvet eyelids

Descend.

Veil

Bastard

As if you were dead

And there was never

Anything you could do

I'm sick on this dull,

Cruel, defeatist attitude

Plague of mine,

Tainted vine,

Your pretense makes

My stomach turn on

A spit. Eating, its

Inside out.

You quit and quit and quit.

Veil

Mirage

The air is dense and thick

Hanging like cotton, filling my lungs

Like neck pillows, my respiratory

Stuffed animal protesting kick;

And I am quick to shut

My eyes to the morning sunlight,

Poured over my head like

Warm orange juice, stinging

I fell asleep in Gods cup; and he is up

The night, in its blind flight disrupt,

I prayed: dissolve, quickly

I knew sleep before

I knew my own mother

And since,

Have been tempted

By its great casuistry.

Veil

Oh, Monster

Be your blackness

Feathery and malignant.

Tickling your insides,

With a turn;

I feel a great weight,

A burn, a bomb

Too aplomb to hide.

Red eye, no less

And even more, in fact

It used to beg to die.

Now it begs to be let

And to get - lord knows

I could bleed out

And haunt this place.

Yet, no one thing

Can handle the weight,

A dense, black mass

Veil

(2)

Of universe potential

Before the big bang.

Let it overhang,

Stretched thin and

Rung of rain.

It has no eyes or ears,

Only a mouth and

Flailing hands, the sour

Breath of death's commands,

Pulling again, always.

Toward, torn;

The dark, the night

Light amnesia morning.

I do not wish to go.

Dead pith, lie low.

You have yours,

Veil

(3)

And yet, rage

Clawing at your

Intestinal jail, hissing;

Spitting through the

Rib cage

evermore.

Veil

Insha'Allah

So far away, like stars

You twinkle, a nightshade

Canopy; someone pulled

The black mesh over our sky

And I wait;

The sun will open his

Great eyelid

Loneliness melts out of

Crevices in my chest

I can breathe, I can see again

Trapped in security, a noose

Dangling, unused.

Thank God,

Veil

Storms

Roll, old man vaporous.

Mass at hand, with

A gloom and a hiss.

Protesting wheels

To the shaky drift.

Inching to the line

Not to be hind,

Lift

And fly above.

Betray it all

At once and

Sans a second thought.

Or glance behind;

Withstanding, you

Came to find

And so cannot.

Veil

Quandary

Fog rolls in and we

Are swimming in milk.

Staring where familiar

Places once were.

As if the crawling clouds

Are uncertainty themselves;

Breath in, sol aerosol,

Diffuse into diffusion

I lose eye and I

Heavy thunderhead.

Sinking, level nigh

Dissolve.

Veil

(A) Part

I heard you filling in cracks;

Retiling and smoothing over.

Only, spilled milk all the time.

You, great fissure, lack;

Create space, breath-

Into that dead mouth, unreceiving.

Sometimes they are lost.

Veil

They Ran

Hard to wake, slow to rise.

Take the sleep from my eyes.

Safe in darkened waves

Where I will stay, our place.

In pictures we are so still;

They lay in wait to lie unseen.

To my face keep looking, I

Knife hollowed lute and

You, bamboo shoot.

Evergreen.

Veil

Stobbit

I still remember exactly.

You wore also, at me.

That jumper, almost

A onesie; those little

Grey boots. Grey boots,

Leaning like you do.

Elbow in hand,

Covering your face.

She was only your mother.

The reason you turned

To me, and turned away.

I looked for you, that day.

I'm certain now I've been in

Love with you ever since.

How afraid I am, how

I cower,

With my prize bleeding

At my feet. You are

Veil

(2)

The sweetest treat,

And my teeth throb,

Little gluttons.

I want to melt from

Each others mouths,

And gush forth, spilling

The insides out, laughing

And painting the walls

With our blood.

Veil

Twister

Time flies up and about

Ever circling, overhead.

Listening,

For the twinkling recollection

Remembered in good detail,

Oh, I'm sure.

Hindsight will tell the future

And pay no mind to present,

Ignoring the ad hoc current,

Contemporary peasant. And

Perhaps it was as was said:

Eye of storm, calm, dead;

Sheppard of vicious winds,

A Saturn of debris; Mercury uncloud

Set us free, now, let it be

Blue sky again.

Veil

Negative

Negate, I've

Negated my life

Neglected the hive

To strive a losing battle

To thrash and gnash and spit

And claw and beat and kick and

Scream like a rabid caged animal

Watching its prey, again, being taken

Away.

Veil

Boga

Mother, I'm sorry

My sinews fail me

I wring my muscles of

Every drop, precious blood

Starving, gasping, failing

I flail;

My legs beg for reprieve

Grip becomes slip

I am losing my shit

Where a werewolf sleeps

Unafraid of day or night

Alike;

Awakened from dream,

Quick to steam,

Born with a thorn

In his side.

Veil

Grandfather

Suffering-Long.

Dragging on and on.

The clock hands

Are slow to stop;

The waves crash

Ever near and always;

The tics drip and

The tocs drop upon

My forehead; Torture.

Anointed. Life and death,

Loss.

The same hourglass.

A sand man sifted

Through dream cloth.

Veil

Beam

Purple powder cast

Into the fire, dancing.

Lovely, scented images

Before me, illusory and

Tempting; the senses in

A body, unrented. Oh,

These empty rooms bray.

Echoes. I long; long

And evermore since the

Day we parted ways.

The lines take shape;

Easy as pi. You again,

How do? Opposite me

on the merry-go-round

Eternally, for now.

Veil

Magpie

Dare I even begin?

To explain;

This visceral rage

I cannot contain.

I forced it upon whom

I thought I knew was

Doomed;

I wanted hellfire;

Area of effect

Them all, me.

Pill-popping makeup

Cakes flaking off

A tortured city wall

In all its fracture could

Not suffice to describe

(2)

Veil

What I read between

Those lines;

Spineless you, discarded gum

Beneath my shoe.

Dreams

Veil

Drowse.

I am slipping,

Melting from top to bottom,

An avalanche of molten skin

I win no longer.

The night has cut my line,

Horizon's razor;

I float into blackness,

Slowly. Disappearing, a body

To the bottom of

The sea; falling from me,

I float for hours.

Whim of mighty way;

Drifting, waiting for day.

Waking up as wet,

I do not know why.

Veil

Relieve

The hot knife in my back.

Slowly twisted at work, aching.

Laid onto the bed, only

My lovers arms hold me closer.

Upon pounds of pillows

The nest is best made

With the wood of elders'

Rest and fade away.

Veil

www.ingramcontent.com/pod-product-compliance
Lightning Source LLC
Chambersburg PA
CBHW070112070426
42448CB00038B/2610